*For Toby,
with very much love.
Thanks for letting me see the world through a kid's eyes again.
Mum*

Scan here to find out more about Australian brush-turkeys (bush-turkeys)

Copyright © 2023 by Ann Göth
All rights reserved.
First published 2023 by Natural Publishing

Website https://anngothauthor.com

No portion of this book may be reproduced in any form without written permission from the author, apart from any fair dealing for the purpose of private study, research, criticism or review, as permitted under the Australian Copyright Act 1968. Enquiries should be made to the author.

Author: Ann Göth
Title: Bush-Turkey Needs a Friend / written & illustrated by Ann Göth
Target Audience: For children
Subjects: Birds - Juvenile Fiction
ISBN: 978-0-6486037-2-6

# Bush-Turkey Needs a Friend

Written and illustrated
by Ann Göth

Natural Publishing

Tom Turkey has hatched
from an egg
deep down in a mound
that is made of leaves and soil.

Tom is all alone.
He does not need his parents.
He is an Australian brush-turkey.
Some people call him bush-turkey.
Tom digs and digs
through all that soil,
up to the sun.

Tom pops out his head.
'Oh,' he thinks,
'I should better be careful,
something is chasing me.'

And he runs as fast as he can
to hide in the bushes.

In the bushes,
Tom finds lots to eat.
Worms and fruit and tiny seeds.

He is happy now with all that
food in his belly.

Tom spreads out his wings
and flaps them really fast.

'Oh,' Tom Turkey thinks,
'I can fly!' and he flies up
a tree to sleep at night.

The morning has arrived.
Tom feels a bit lonely now.
He wants to find a friend.

He looks down from his tree.
What does he see?

'Hello, I'm Tom,'
Tom says, 'and who are you?'
'I am Debby Duckling,'
the little duck says.
'And over there is my mum,
she looks after me.'
'I don't know my mother,' Tom says.
'I don't need looking after.'

'You are a strange bird,' Debby says.
'You are not a duck,'
and Debby waddles away.

Tom walks further.
Who is this?
'Hello, I'm Tom,' Tom says,
'and who are you?'
'I'm Erik Emu,' Erik says,
'and back there is my dad,
he looks after me.'
'I don't know my dad,' Tom says,
'I can live on my own.'

'You are a strange bird,'
Erik says.
'You are not an emu.'
And Erik walks away.

Who is this? Could this be a friend?
'Hello, I'm Tom,' Tom now says,
'and who are you?'
'I'm Lara Lapwing,' Lara says,
'and this is my nest,
where I hatched from my egg.'

Tom is thinking hard now.
'My nest was a mound,' he says,
'and there was soil all around me.'

'You are strange', Lara says.
'You can't be a lapwing.'
And Lara runs away.

Tom walks to a farm.
He meets a little chicken.
'Hello, I'm Tom,' Tom says,
'and who are you?'
'I'm Cleo Chicken,' Cleo says.
Tom looks at her.
'I look much like you, Cleo,'
Tom says.
'Do you want to be my friend?'
'I can't be your friend,' Cleo says.
'You are different in colour to me.'
And Cleo walks away.

Tom sits down and thinks.
He is different from other birds.
No father, no mother,
no nest, different colour.
Maybe he is the only turkey
in the world? Can you guess
how lonely he feels?

So he lives by himself
for many days.

He grows and grows into a big brush-turkey with strong legs and big feet.

His head is red like an apple, his neck yellow as the sun. And what's that around his neck? A long yellow wattle that dangles back and forth.

One day, Tom feels lonely again,
but he can't find a friend.
So Tom plays raking by himself.
With his big, strong feet,
he rakes all the leaves and soil
into a big, big mound,
much bigger than he is!

But who is this?
There is another bird!
'Hello you,'
Tom now says,
'I'm Tom,
and who are you?'
'I'm Tina Turkey,' Tina says,
'And I look so much like you,
you must be a brush-turkey too!'

Tina climbs up Tom's mound
and digs a deep
hole into it.

But she is not happy.
'It's not warm enough
for my egg', Tina says.
And Tina walks away.

Tom feels lonely again.
He wants his mound to be
warm so Tina will return.
One day, the sun shines,
and he opens up the mound so
the sun can make it really warm.

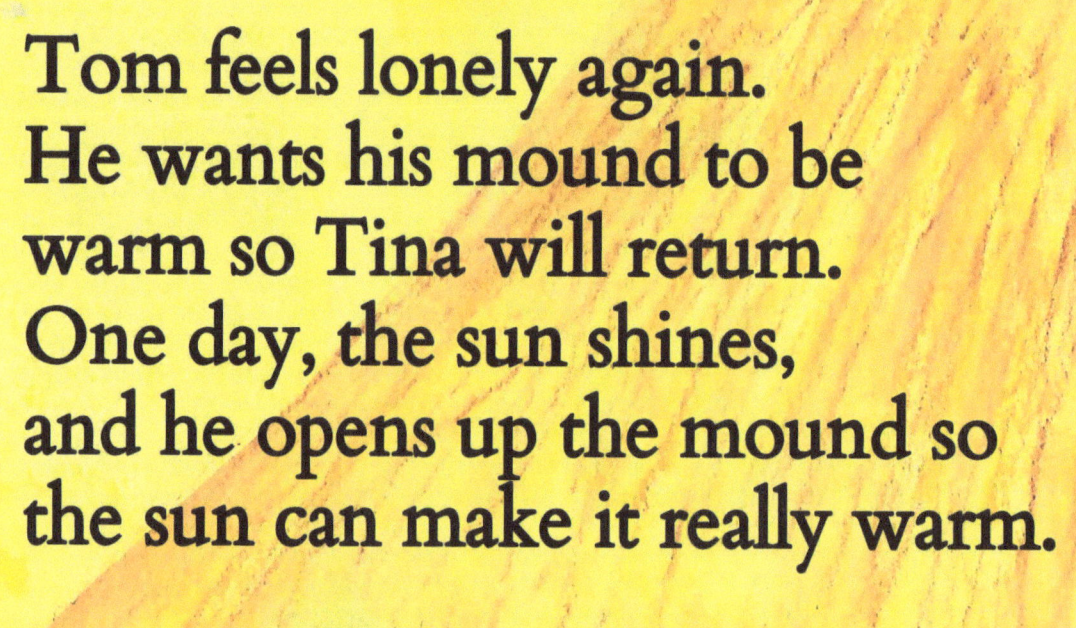

When the rain comes,
he rakes leaves onto the mound
so the water will run down and
not cool the mound down again.
Every day, Tom looks after his mound,
and he waits for Tina to return.

There she is!
Tina has returned!
She digs a hole
into the mound,
and she is happy now!

'This is nice and warm
for my egg,' Tina says,
and she lays her white egg
into the hole,
deep down in the mound.

The sun goes down;
it is getting dark.
Tom and Tina fly up a tree,
and they sit together
during the night.

'I'm happy now,' Tom says,
'I found a friend,
and I have got a mound.'

'I am not strange,' Tom thinks.
'I'm just a little different
to the other birds!'

# About the Bush-Turkey

The correct name for these unique birds is Australian brush-turkey, but many people call them bush-turkeys. They are native to the East Coast of Australia.

Unlike their avian counterparts, brush-turkeys do not incubate their eggs by sitting on them. Instead, they utilize the heat generated from compost mounds to warm the eggs. The males are responsible for constructing these mounds and meticulously monitor the temperature daily using a sensor located in their beak. They maintain the necessary temperature by adding or removing nesting material as needed.

The females lay large eggs, which result in well-developed chicks. However, they do not provide any parental care after hatching. The chicks, born within the mounds, do not form any bonds with their parents and are independent from the moment they hatch, a characteristic that sets these birds apart.

Brush-turkeys have recently been spotted in numerous suburbs where they had not been seen for many years, particularly in Sydney. Their presence has sparked interest among both children and adults, leading to a desire to learn more about them. This book aims to cater to that curiosity.

*Scan here to find out more about brush-turkeys*

## About the Author

Dr. Ann Göth has studied Australian brush-turkeys for over 20 years. She frequently shares her knowledge and insights through Australian newspapers, radio broadcasts, and local council meetings. As a science teacher, she takes great pleasure in introducing young minds to the marvels of the natural world.

www.ingramcontent.com/pod-product-compliance
Lightning Source LLC
Chambersburg PA
CBHW041200290426
44109CB00002B/85